CW01302548

Copyright © 2023 Wynn D. Day All rights reserved

No part of this book may be reproduced, or stored in a retrieval system, or transmitted in any form or by any means, electronic, mechanical, photocopying, recording, or otherwise, without express written permission of the publisher.

All poems by Wynn D. Day

Just for Kicks ... Kings & Queens

by Wynn D. Day

Kings and Queens from 1066

- WILLIAM THE CONQUEROR (1066- 1087)
- WILLIAM II (1087 – 1100)
- HENRY I (1100 - 1135)
- STEPHEN (1135 - 1154)
- HENRY II (1154 - 1189)
- RICHARD I (1189 - 1199)
- JOHN (1199 - 1216)
- HENRY III (1216 - 1272)
- EDWARD I (1272 - 1307)
- EDWARD II (1307 - 1327)
- EDWARD III (1327 - 1377)
- RICHARD II (1377 - 1399)
- HENRY IV (1399 - 1413)
- HENRY V (1413 - 1422)
- HENRY VI (1422 - 1461 and 1470 - 1471)
- EDWARD IV (1461 - 1470 and 1471 - 1483)
- EDWARD V (Apr-Jun 1483)
- RICHARD III (1483 - 1485)
- HENRY VII (1485 - 1509)
- HENRY VIII (1509 - 1547)
- EDWARD VI (1547 - 1553)
- MARY I (1553 - 1558)
- ELIZABETH I (1558 - 1603)
- JAMES I (1603 - 1625)
- CHARLES I (1625 - 1649)
- CHARLES II (1660 - 1685)
- JAMES II (1685 - 1688)
- WILLIAM III (1689 - 1702) and MARY II (1689 - 1694)
- ANNE (1702 - 1714)
- GEORGE I (1714 - 1727)
- GEORGE II (1727 - 1760)
- GEORGE III (1760 - 1820)
- GEORGE IV (1820 - 1830)
- WILLIAM IV (1830 - 1837)
- VICTORIA (1837 - 1901)
- EDWARD VII (1901 - 1910)
- GEORGE V (1910 - 1936)

- EDWARD VIII (June - Dec 1936)
- GEORGE VI (1936 - 1952)
- ELIZABETH II (1952 - 2022)
- CHARLES III (2022 - present)

WILLIAM THE CONQUEROR (1066 - 1087)

When the Bayeux Tapestry was being sewn

I thought that England was the place to own.

So from Normandy, on my ship,

Like Haley's comet, I made my trip

To take on Harold on the beach,

Across La Manche so I could reach

Hastings, and make it mine,

For my glorious battle on the shoreline.

WILLIAM II (1087 - 1100)

This second Billy, known as red,

Did not have the fortune to die in bed.

He went out hunting in the forest new,

But his assassin knew what to do.

Was it by order of his brother Hal,

Who sent Walter Tyrel, as his pal,

To shoot poor Willy in the back

So he could get the monarchy back on track?

HENRY I (1100 - 1135)

"Please oh please get for me

A dish – a surfeit of lamprey.

Send it up to Henry Beauclerk,

While I wait impatiently in the dark.

And if for this I do not survive,

Make sure my Reading monks will thrive.

Then send me there so I may rest.

Please do these things at my behest."

STEPHEN (1135 - 1154)

If Steve had drowned with Bill Adelin,

Matilda's son wouldn't have to win

The throne, from old cross eyed Steve,

And she would never have had to believe,

That the crown should have passed to her.

For the nobles would just not concur

That women had a right to the throne.

So Stephen got it – he didn't moan!

HENRY II (1154 - 1189)

When Matty's son Henry made his claim,

He married Eleanor of fair Aquitaine.

They had a troublesome brood of kids

Who with their mum wanted to be rid

Of poor old Hal! His mate Thomas Becket

Also caused him grief. His end was met

By the arrival of the four knights,

After this Henry's life was full of strife.

RICHARD I (1189 - 1199)

My name is Richard the Lionheart.

When papa died, I decided to start

My reign, by going on the third crusade.

And in my battles against Saladin, I made

Many victories, with Queen Berengaria at my side

Triumphantly through middle-eastern lands we'd ride.

And when I was captured sweet Blondel

Would sing his songs, and all was well.

JOHN (1199 - 1216)

King John - the king who was nefarious

Took the crown jewels where it was precarious.

So bad was he, the barons did indeed

Take wicked John off to Runymede.

For the Magna Carta – which he had to sign,

To reassure the barons he was not malign.

But he stole the crown from his killed nephew,

What'ere he did, this king could n'er be true.

HENRY III (1216 - 1272)

Hal number three was but a boy,

When he was the youngest roi.

He was fond of raising taxes,

But the height of his climaxes

Was his fight with Simon De Montford

When his son Eddy held the sword.

His reign ended with quite a wham

When Simon was killed at Evesham!

EDWARD I (1272 - 1307)

Eddy one was the Scots hammer.

But his real claim to glamour

Were the castles he built in Wales,

Effective defences; effective gaols.

Mr Longshanks – moody and tall,

He was responsible for Wallace's fall.

But with his reputation set,

A warrior, as good as we could get.

EDWARD II (1307 - 1327)

Eddy two with his friend Piers,

Caused much trouble and many fears.

His friendship led to his deposition,

But wilful Eddy had no contrition.

With a troubled kingdom he would call a truce,

But in Scotland they had Robert the Bruce.

So he was sent to Berkeley Castle,

And put to death, to save the hassle.

EDWARD III (1327 - 1377)

Edward three was good and able –

The king who made King Arthur's table.

Both he and his wife Pippa,

Knocked out far too many a nipper,

Which caused a lot of future trouble

Which was the Wars of the Roses bubble.

It never burst for many a year,

And really cost the country dear.

RICHARD II (1377 - 1399)

Richard's father was the Black Prince,

Not destined for his kingship since

A dose of dysentery took his life,

And left his son with all the strife.

The peasant's revolt and hundred year's war,

Helped spoil his reign, that's for sure.

Then up to Pontefract – but not for cakes,

For sheer incompetence his life they take.

HENRY IV (1399 - 1413)

Henry four was into theft,

He stole the crown while Richard slept.

Fed up of Dick's ineptitude,

Dick's crown and life did not include

His wicked cousin barging in

To take the throne away from him.

But Henry's life was full of worry,

So his son took over in a hurry.

HENRY V (1413 - 1422)

Henry five – now here's his story,

He had a reign all clothed in glory.

He won the battle of Agincourt,

To show us what a king is for.

Then he married the princess of France

To give glorious England the chance,

To rule both kingdoms through his son,

But inherited madness must be overcome.

HENRY VI (1422 - 1461 & 1470 - 1471)

I am poor King Henry six.

I'm sick of people playing tricks

And urging me to go to war

To keep my thrones – but what for?

Wife Margaret spitting in my ear,

"Come on, come on…" but I fear

Cousin Eddy coming after me,

I wish they all would leave me be…

EDWARD IV (1461 - 1470 & 1471 - 1483)

Edward four was very tall,

His mother's husband was very small.

He had a warrior-like tendency,

So decided to try for his ascendancy.

He pinched the crown from Henry six,

But found that Towton was his fix.

And through his daughter Liz of York.

The Tudor line became a fork.

EDWARD V (Apr - Jun 1483)

Edward five went to the Tower,

He never got a sniff of power.

Torn away from his mother's arms,

With brother Rich he came to harm.

It wasn't till Chas number two

That anybody had a clue,

When they dug and found remains,

And Uncle Richard took the blame.

RICHARD III (1483 - 1485)

Richard three with crooked spine

Had an interesting time.

Stealing thrones and killing kids –

No wonder they wanted to be rid.

So off he went to Bosworth field,

But then he went and lost his steed.

Then Henry seven made his mark,

And Dick was left under the car park.

HENRY VII (1485 - 1509)

Hal seven as a king was wiser,

He was known for being a miser.

His mother Mags pushed him on,

And when he had the battle won,

He married Liz to join the lines,

And then his reign would work out fine.

He worked hard – and with this context

Look at who was coming next!

HENRY VIII (1509 - 1547)

Henry the eighth with his six wives –

All of them had rotten lives.

Beheading, divorcing, dying and such –

He plundered the churches, but didn't have much

Time for matters of state. He was too busy

Trying to get himself a son, but he got Lizzy!

His jousting accident helped make him obese,

Then mood swings and ulcers led to his decease.

EDWARD VI (1547 - 1553)

The throne came to Edward as a boy,

Throughout his time a regency was employed.

He wanted to change the rule of succession,

And then his sisters he didn't mention.

He left the throne to Lady Jane Grey,

And she became Queen for just nine days.

At fifteen Edward died of T B,

But trouble came after – you'll see!

MARY I (1553 - 1558)

"My name is Mary of the bloody sort,

There'll be no protestants at my court!

Get those fires lit straight away,

Do it now, hear what I say!"

Philip of Spain came to crack the whip,

But no babies – so he returned to his ship.

He left her lonely, sick and ill,

She died soon after – by God's will.

ELIZABETH I (1558 - 1603)

Here's our famous Elizabeth the first.

With a husband she was never cursed.

Clever, wily; she was justly proud

Of her speeches with the crowd,

Who loved the Shakespeare, prosperity, peace,

And prayed her reign would never cease.

She was our wonderful virgin queen,

The likes of which have ne're been seen.

JAMES I (1603 - 1625)

Her successor was the first King Jim,

Mary of Scot's son – that was him.

His mother killed, but he was heir,

So he left for England and he lived there.

Not a handsome man it's true,

He was okay – he knew what to do.

The gunpowder plot was foiled,

So his reign was never spoiled.

CHARLES I (1625 - 1649)

His wife was Henrietta Maria,

But Chaz one thought he was higher

Than King of his people. He thought

He was more than mere mortals who ought

To let him do just as he pleased.

But out of his Kingship he was soon squeezed.

Then off to the block wearing two shirts

To chop off his head. Bet that hurt!

CHARLES II (1660 - 1685)

For Charlie two the throne's restoration

Was very welcome after his vacation.

He'd had to wait for Oli to die,

To commission crown jewels for him to try.

Louise, Barbara and sweet Nell Gwynne,

For his pleasure – they waited for him.

The plague and fire were during his reign,

But to get him a son, all was in vain.

JAMES II (1685 - 1688)

Mr Trouble, how James two should be known,

He was a Catholic when he came to the throne.

The people and nobles were all in fear,

But all their complaints he did not hear.

Wife Mary's baby in a warming pan,

Made the succession a different plan.

With Glorious revolution on his hands,

James was deprived of all his lands.

WILLIAM III (1689 - 1702) &
MARY II (1689 - 1694)

They've invited me and my husband Bill

Over to England, the throne to fill.

They've sent my dad over to France

To live with King Louis and give him a chance.

"The little gentleman in the black waistcoat" toast,

Would have been what would have hurt me the most!

We did our best; we both tried,

But I left first, of the pox I died.

ANNE (1702 - 1714)

Poor unlucky, old Queen Anne,

Tries for an heir as much as she can.

Eighteen pregnancies all failed and doomed,

A new royal house for her then loomed.

For her – The Act of Union – a single state,

And meeting Sarah Churchill was her fate.

The Old Pretender's claim was big,

But the Hanovarians got the gig.

GEORGE I (1714 - 1727)

Now look at German George the first.

He came to England – what a curse!

He spoke no English, but had the power

To lock up his poor wife in a tower.

Son and father hate each other –

Because his dad locked up his mother.

He was a poor start for the George's.

A legacy of hopelessness he forges!

GEORGE II (1727 - 1760)

George two, arrogant and smart,

Put the George's reputation in the cart.

He wasn't friends with his son Fred,

Who died suddenly in his bed.

Bonnie Prince Charlie came to depose,

But he failed, as everyone knows.

Fond of protesting his Englishness.

He wasn't. But we couldn't care less!

GEORGE III (1760 - 1820)

George the third, long lived and mad,

Was a prolific sort of dad.

And with revolution in France,

He knew that there was a chance

That America would go the same way.

And of course there came the day,

When mad old George would lose it all.

And tubby George four got the call.

GEORGE IV (1820 - 1830)

When the throne came to fat George four,

He proved to everyone he could eat more.

He ruined his marriage with a tryst

With Mrs Firzherbert –what a hedonist!

He went to Brighton for a major build –

His Pavilions with fine stuff was filled.

Then overeating, and as his button popped –

Gluttony over – to death he dropped.

WILLIAM IV (1830 - 1837)

Sailor Bill, fourth of this realm,

Was judged too stupid to take the helm

On the ships he liked to sail –

The last of George three's brood to prevail.

He freed the slaves and helped the poor,

But what else he did, I'm not too sure.

He hung on till Vicki came of age,

To take her from her mother's cage.

VICTORIA (1837 - 1901)

I am the Queen, and I'm not amused,

I will not have my word abused,

By all my squabbling children here,

But I wish I had my Albert near.

When he died I had little hope,

And till John Brown I didn't cope.

My time here just goes on and on.

I've had enough; I wish I was gone.

EDWARD VII (1901 - 1910)

"My mother said, I'm not good enough.

But I'm likeable, affable and not so tough.

I'm fond of going out to play

With Alice Kepple and friends most days.

I have royal relatives all over the place,

And as Emperor I hold the mace.

But as King – there weren't so many years,

And I didn't fulfil my mother's fears!"

GEORGE V (1910 - 1936)

It was much to his surprise,

'Cause to the sea he had his ties.

On the death of brother Eddy

George was king, but he wasn't ready.

Then he married his sister in law,

But to rescue Tsar Nicky he wasn't sure.

Then he worried about his errant son

And so he should – God's will be done!

EDWARD VIII (June - Dec 1936)

"I'm Eddy eight, and I'll decide

If I'd rather run and hide,

Or keep with me my lovely Wallis,

I love her so – she is my solace.

I don't think I will be King,

All that work – and not a thing

That is pleasant for me.

I'm off to France, so leave me be."

GEORGE VI (1936 - 1952)

Ed left the crown – with hearts a flutter,

To his brother – who had a stutter.

Dependable, shy and full of doubt,

How good he was, we soon found out.

He saw us through World War two,

Along with Churchill his stature grew.

He helped to make the monarchy strong,

Though when he died he was quite young.

ELIZABETH II (1952 - 2022)

Elizabeth two – for seventy years,

Has shown us what is needed here.

Through all the times bad and good,

She's been the best, just like she should.

Her children at times, have caused her strife,

But she's persevered throughout her life,

To show us what a good queen should be.

So cheers to the Queen- of the land of the free.

CHARLES III (2022 - present)

When Charlie took over he was quite old,

He'd lost Diana and nearly his soul.

Later he made Camilla his Queen,

This is what should always have been.

It was Andrew first, who caused much trouble,

Then Harry joined in to make it double.

Chas is doing his best, but we don't know whether

He'll be able to hold everything together.

Printed in Great Britain
by Amazon